The Wind Of Change

The Wind Of Change

A record of Spiritual Dialogues

Channelled by Julie Soskin

Ashgrove Press, Bath

Published in Great Britain by
ASHGROVE PRESS LIMITED
7 Locksbrook Road Estate
Bath BA1 3DZ

First Ashgrove Press edition 1994
Reprinted 1996

ISBN 1 85398-075-7

Original material channelled by Julie Soskin
with the assistance of Jenny Grant

Original manuscript edited by Jean and Roy Simpson
Cover designed by Rupert Soskin, Lion Studios, Hampton, Middlesex

Printed and bound in the United Kingdom by
Redwood Books, Trowbridge, Wilts

ACKNOWLEDGEMENTS

My warmest thanks go to Jenny Grant, whose Light
very strong. Without her collaboration, this channellin
would not have been possible.

My appreciation also goes to Roy and Jean Simpson wh
edited the original material faithfully without changing it
substance.

To Jane and David Bowles, who believed in the material.

And to Rupert, my husband, who illustrated the cover anc
who taught me the true meaning of love.

PREFACE TO THE NEW EDITION

When I first began channelling back in 1989, I had no thoughts of turning the information I was being given into a book. When *The Wind of Change* was published the following year I would never have believed this would run to a second edition. The response to both this book and its sequel *The Cosmic Dance*, has been nothing short of phenomenal. I would like to thank everyone who has written to me with their kind words and positive thoughts.

There are many stories surrounding the publication of these books which, for me, are touched with magic. On the very same day the manuscript of *The Cosmic Dance* was dispatched to the publishers, I was given a leaflet which contained excerpts from someone else's channelling. I was stunned when I saw how similar these were to parts of *The Cosmic Dance*. In some places even the same phrases had been used! When I turned to the back page I was further amazed to discover the channeller lived in the USA! This served not only to confirm the truth of what I had been channelling, but has also made me aware that the messages coming through are doing so on a global level.

Six months after the publication of *The Wind of Change*, I received a phone call from a medium who lives in Manchester. She told me that back in 1985 she had begun to receive information about the coming changes. She was told, by her spiritual communicators, to look out for a book which was shortly to be published, which described these changes. She was even given the title of the book - *The Wind of Change!* Apparently she drove her family to distraction searching for this book, and only found it when she saw it reviewed in *Psychic News*. She has no doubts this is the book she was told about. This story is truly amazing because in 1985 I had not even begun my channelling - *The Wind of Change* was started in January 1990. Also, it was the February storms, which raged during the channelling sessions and sounded so loud on the tapes, which gave me the inspiration to call this book *The Wind of Change*. In my husband's words - "You have to take your hat off to the organisers!".

On a personal level I have now committed myself totally to the integration of my soul on all levels. Some of the experiences I have been through, during the process of my release, have been extremely uncomfortable. I am not so foolish as to believe I have finished my growth, for this is, as I understand it, a never ending process. But I do believe I have jettisoned my fear on an emotional level, and in doing so I have found a stillness, for which I am very thankful. Needless to say, the nature of my work has changed. But I always endeavour, when asked, to help open the doors to others.

One of the many letters I have received was from Sir George Trevelyan, whom I had never met nor spoken to before. He has been most encouraging, and kindly wrote the forward to *The Cosmic Dance*. I am grateful to Sir George for his support, and to all others who know we are truly through the barriers now.

Since *The Wind of Change* was first published many new things have been revealed to me, and I truly know that our long held aspirations to the higher levels of understanding are now finally being realised. I wish you all great joy.

JULIE SOSKIN

INTRODUCTION

I first became aware of my psychic abilities at the age of four when I realized I was able to perceive things that others could not. As a teenager I developed the disconcerting ability to read other people's minds as clearly as a telex. Naturally, this trait did not endear me greatly to others. I instinctively knew I couldn't discuss this with my family or friends, and although I was happy for the greater part of my formative years, I felt apart from others.

In 1974, I became fascinated by the Tarot and meditated on the Major Arcana as a means of enhancing my self-awareness. Soon friends began asking me to lay spreads for them. As I had had no training I decided to join a development group run by a lady from the local Spiritualist church. Later I went on to study at the College of Psychic Studies in London, and eventually became one of the College's own mediums.

Before long I was running my own awareness and healing groups. I have always seen spiritual healing as essential and integral to the work of clairvoyance. My work gives me immense happiness and satisfaction.

Although I worked with 'guides' in the traditional sense, I was never aware of them as distinct personalities - rather as different levels of energy that, thanks to my disciplined training, I could tap into and access.

One day last year I was idly laying out a Tarot spread for myself - something which I rarely do, when I was astonished to see I had drawn the Tower card in the first position. I laid them out again - and drew the same card! I felt this to be most odd and put them away in a gesture of denial. Four days later curiosity prompted me to try again. The Tower reappeared. I did it once more, shuffling thoroughly first, and it appeared for the fourth consecutive time. This time I could not deny it.

The Tower is tradittionaly the card of destruction, revolution and revelation, suggesting some huge, momentous life-shifts. I realised later that the disruption and illumination was a reference to my inner, rather than my outer life! I became aware of a shift in the psychic energies within myself. I no longer felt as though I was simply linking to my spirit guides, but to what I can only describe as a 'Light force'.

At this time so many different messages and prediction of gloom, doom, ecological disaster and Armageddon were coming to me from all areas, I felt I must find my own truth.

My friend and colleague Jenny Grant offered to help, and we set aside a regular session each week to find the highest level of truth. Two weeks into the work, the Berlin Wall came down. People were on the move, and there was a definite feeling of urgency and acceleration on all levels.

I channelled the material, and Jenny asked the questions and recorded the responses. During the first session she asked from whom or what the information was coming. "A synthesis of energies of higher consciousness - 'Original Thought'" - was the reply. As time went on we were told a book would be dictated that would tell humanity about the important time of transition the world was now facing.

In February 1990 we were in the middle of the dictation when the terrible storms came, and on tape was recorded the sound of the hurricane-force winds that threatened to raise our roof. "The Wind of Change" was the obvious title for this book.

During the sessions I experienced the sensation of a great power entering my body, and in my mind's eye I saw the sword of power and truth and the orb of wisdom. Sometimes, my body was left tingling, as if with an electric current. The book took ten session to complete. Interestingly, there have been no barriers to publishing this book. It has come about with tremendous ease and rapidity, with no sense of effort on my part.

Increasingly, I now work on a 'soul-level', which helps people to awaken to their own spiritual being, of which I find more and more people are becoming aware. I do not feel special in any way. As the book says, "All will lead, and all will serve", but I feel I can open doors for others, and I hope this book will make people think more deeply about themselves and the part they have to play in the Universe.

Every single person is important, every single person matters. We are all facing profound changes, inner and outer, and I believe the underlying purpose of this process is to convince mankind finally that we are divine creatures in essence, spirit encased in matter - and that we can all aspire to the Christ consciousness, the level of higher understanding.

JULIE SOSKIN
Teddington, June 1990.

I. THE TRANSITION

The world was created by a thought; the Universe was created by a thought. Forever there has been Original Thought, this energy that you may call God, but which is not as you understand God to be. You may call it Consciousness, but it is not as you understand consciousness to be. It is in simple terms a thought. The thought is made up of particles and the thought created the Universe by the explosion of these particles or some of the particles emerging from the whole. When this occurred the particles were set free. The particles were then left alone to experience many different things in different galaxies, worlds and levels. But the thought, the whole, was still there, because the expulsion of the particles did not diminish the thought itself. It is to that pure thought, pure consciousness, to pure God that you are linked.

This world, your world is Light. It began in Light, its essence is Light and at this time Light will emerge triumphant. We do not mean that this will be a fight between good and evil, and in giving you all this information we will try to break down the preconception of these ideas.

Your world and other worlds were created by the thought. It was Light and the Light shone everywhere. Over periods of time (time is not an accurate way of describing this, but we use the word so that you can understand), the thought and the Light gradually evolved into matter. As you know, the world began as a living, breathing planet long before animal and human life was on it. It is still a living, breathing Light.

Man evolved on it in many ways, with greater strengths than are to be found in other 'worlds' because he developed to varying degrees different areas of his being. He developed physical strength. He also grew a mental capacity, an intellect which created a scientific approach. He developed emotionally and spiritually. You are unique, because in other places life evolved differently, in only one or two areas of being, whereas you grew in several areas. These different areas of evolution not only gave you strengths, but also gave you great dilemmas because they often worked against each other - the intellect fighting with the emotions, the emotions fighting with the spirit, and all these things affecting the physical. However, you have evolved now to a degree that brings you to the present important transition.

It is, we know, the transition that you are most interested in. There is no single reason for it. However you had evolved, there would be a transition on your globe at this time, so to say it is a judgement of God or because you have done ill to your planet is not true, although these things did not help your Earth. Your globe has simply come to the end of a cycle of being. Since a fair percentage of the population has risen in consciousness, they will meet the demands of the transition. But the changes coming (on a physical and global level - we emphasize this) would still be taking place if your planet was devoid of all life. It is a changeover of energies, not just for your planet but in universal and cosmic proportions. Your science is still in its early days but it is developed enough for your scientists to recognise the changes very clearly in the coming months and years.

A similar transition has in fact happened to your world before. It occurred at a time when people were already inhabiting this globe but it affected fewer people because the world was not as densely populated then. It is not right for people to perceive this transition as 'Judgement Day', as 'Armageddon' or as the 'Hand and Wrath of God'. These terms mislead. (We must say now that some of these words are not fully explanatory of what is happening. We try to give the words that will be understood, and that are nearest to the truth, but some elements of the truth are beyond your comprehension and beyond the description of words. However, we aim to be as accurate and as clear as possible.)

There is talk of a 'wind of change'. This is a useful way of describing the transition - a universal wind that is blowing. There is an ebbing and flowing of all energies. Original thought is never destroyed but it moulds and forms other energies as it progresses and evolves. The wind of change is coming and is almost on your planet. The original energy turning itself into something else. We use again the analogy that you well understand, of the caterpillar emerging as the butterfly. There will be destruction, and destruction is nothing new to your planet; there will be violence, and there will be what are called natural disasters. Many lives will disappear from your globe, and most of these will not reincarnate.

Not all enlightened or evolved souls will complete this transition. There will be some, a few, whose work here is done, and they will go with the souls that leave in order to help them. That is their new work. But on the whole, because of the sensitivity of the souls that have evolved, developing intuition and psychic ability, they will know instinctively where to be and what to do and so they will survive.

It is important that there is no fear. Fear brings destruction and you have already realized this. The evolved souls will lose their fear, and fear is the major element that must be worked on in the next few years.

Fear must go.

It is this development that is needed most. Individuals can be helped by others, but it is within their own being that they must let go of fear completely and rise to the next stage of development for the human race. It is an opportunity for all. No one is excluded, but time is running out and people must move fast. We know that some will not accomplish the task, but there is a proportion of individuals who have a very real chance, a very real opportunity to complete the transformation, and that is what you are seeing now. You are witnessing evolution accelerating in a way much faster than at the previous great transition. It has never been experienced in such an accelerated form. You can help and these words can help.

The other major change for the individual to accomplish at this time is the dying away of the outer image, the personality, the ego. This information itself will bring some alarm. People will feel that their personality is a necessity. It is not, and it must be thrown aside.

Already there have been major developments within the individual. The year just gone (1989) has seen tremendous acceleration of the process and in the next year or two up until 1992/3 you will see an enormous rate of progress within individuals who can transform themselves - but this will also mean that the difference between them and those who are lower in the evolutionary cycle is more marked.

Unfortunately the further you progress the less you will be able to help those who withdraw into the misery of their fear. Each teacher, each master of souls is not far enough beyond his pupils in progress to be able to do so; that is the way it is and must be. So for some more advanced individuals it will be almost impossible to touch those who are very despondent with the weight of their fear, their personality and their ego. But for those who are closer to you, you can help by your words, by your energy, by your Light.

However, you must first lose the desire to help, for it will of itself hinder your actual help for others. The knowing of what to do will help. The desire, the remnant of your personality, your ego, must be let go. Also, dear children of this precious Earth, some of you will know that there are people around you whom you cannot help at all. You must accept this. It is not possible to help everyone.

There is a purple aura of Light around your globe. There are also dark, black areas; but the purple, protective Light will save the world itself from utter destruction. You are privileged, dear children of this Earth; you have a precious gift - the gift of life - and those living at this time dwell perhaps in the most precious time of all on your globe. Those of you who have prayed, sent Light, healed the world, will live to see the day when some degree of peace and perfection will prevail. You are privileged - not elite, but privileged - to be here at this time.

The world and the Universe watch with interest, and yes, you are being watched by beings from other worlds who realise what is happening to your globe and understand what is happening to theirs; but with your globe there is a marked change - more marked than with any other. Some of you dear children of Earth have seen and felt these beings. They are fascinated by you, they delight in you, they are interested by you, because you are not like them, and through you in this transition they will further understand themselves and the way they are. You have the ability to be a balanced force in the Universe, balanced in a way that no other planet approaches, and that is what is transpiring: a balance of Light and dark.

So far you have lived to a large degree by the laws of cause and effect. But we tell you now with certainty that this will come to an end. There will be individuals who will deny it, even advanced people, who are unfortunately having to set the pattern of denial because of the original emanation that they follow genetically. But it is the truth.

There will be a balancing of energy and then the energy will turn to Light. There will be no darkness on your globe. Even the days will be affected. Your sun is changing, and in a short space of time there will be another source of Light. Consequently there will be no day or night but there will be permanent Light, and to a large degree your planet will have a permanent temperature - a moderate temperature which will in itself force evolution.

Be aware, dear children of this Earth, that this transition exists in reality and those who doubt will have no doubt in the next year or two as they see the changes occurring. You must have no fear or sadness for those who will not in physical terms survive the transition. Every individual has an energy. That energy is what you call the soul. Your souls are energy. It is that energy that never dies. It is that energy which, when the body dies, goes into what you define as Spirit. That energy is not destroyed but will journey on. Some will mingle in Spirit as a kind of group energy which in itself will change. Others will, in your terms, reincarnate in another world; they will not reincarnate in yours.

Within three to five years at the most there will be scientific proof of the energy that you call your soul. You can clearly understand that you do not see energy. You only see energy where it transfers into some kind of matter, and it is the physical matter of the body that is seen, not the energy that is within. The scientists talk of energy in biological terms and there is a biological energy, but it is not that of which we speak. It is the energy that you call your soul which is present from the beginning of your life to the end. What happens at your death is similar to the shelling of a pea - and the soul moves on.

It is the soul that is your individual truth. Each soul has a different level of energy; each soul has its own Light. There is, dear children, no darkness of the soul. This is an illusion given out by people who have lived by fear, who were prepared to exploit that fear in order to control. There is in reality no darkness of any soul. There is a different level of energy but no darkness. The darkness comes from the negative mind and energy generated within the individual. This hampers the soul but it can never destroy it.

We speak now of the way in which negative energy and thought created disharmony and have disseminated it in your globe. There is a destructive force of energy that has been formed out of the minds of men. If you can imagine the negative thoughts like little crystals of darkness in your atmosphere then you can begin to see how a large number of these negative crystals join together, as it were, from individuals, and en masse they create a disturbance - or, in your words, evil. This for example happened very clearly in your last World War when these negative crystals joined together to allow individuals who would never have thought of it within themselves, to destroy, to torture and be cruel to people of a race they decided to hate.

But evil cannot exist without the thoughts of men. Most of the life forces from other worlds do not even comprehend the concept of good and evil. It is largely a human perception, contorted and confused from early times. The negative traits developed, became accentuated and are now a big problem for you all, so that you have enormous challenges in front of you - but we hope and expect you to take this leap in understanding.

It is very important at this time that there is full comprehension of what the soul is. Greater understanding of this energy will promote evolution and will make it possible for those of intellectual and high mental capacity to jettison their fear; this is coming soon. Science plays a part in this transition. It will play a part in the knowledge that is coming of the energy force within the body which you call the soul. It will play a part in the work it is doing on what you call "time". It is very difficult to explain to people who have lived by this linear element that it really does not exist as you know it. This is a difficult concept to break down; in many ways more difficult than that of the soul. But it will come about.

We must spend a few more words on fear. The insertion of fear into the human make-up came about very early on in your evolution. There was implanted in early man an enormously strong instinct for survival which was needed at that point. Instead of disappearing as it should have done when it became unnecessary, this element increased, bringing about wars, fighting and strife. When you converse with and relate to another individual you are in contact with another part of yourself. Each soul, each energy is individual but it is part of a whole. Early man ignored this truth and saw as separate, as evil, that which he was not prepared to understand. His excessive fear intensified the negative particles in the atmosphere, which were used by bands of individuals not evil in themselves, but caught up in their own negativity. As a result, there has been much destruction.

When there is violence and destruction it is also destruction of part of the individual who inflicts it. That is why the laws of cause and effect have worked - not as retribution, not as judgement, but because the individual inflicted the pain on himself which bound him within himself and manifested in his own life: that is how it worked. It is enormously difficult for some of you to free yourselves from this genetic flaw, bred over generations and ruling you by fear and hatred, but it is a real possibility at this time. It is only because of the present transition that this possibility exists. We urge you children of Earth - take this opportunity. You won't stop evolving, but you will hinder your growth if you don't take it.

There is a force field of Light that can pull you up and dissolve the darkness within. You are, as it were, climbing a big mountain; the end is not quite yet in sight, but you know you are near. Children of Earth, we ask you to look at yourselves, we ask you to feel the Light and truth and to stop making excuses. We ask you not because it affects the power and the energy that we come from: we ask you for yourselves.

Your excuses are made out of fear by a very devious turn of the mind. Your conscious mind wants to see things, as you term it, 'in black and white'. When it is met with information that it cannot put into these categories it instantly disregards them or makes excuses. This is one element. There is another. You humans are very good at making excuses out of laziness, out of fear of what is truth and what must be done. We give you an example. A mother, over-restrictive of a child, restricts it and then makes the excuse, "It's only because I want to protect you. I want to make you happy." This is an excuse because the mother does not want to lose the child. The world is full of excuses and it is these that must be looked at.

Your globe is a paradise, truly was a paradise and it truly will be again. You are seeing a break-down of structures and restrictions, alarming to many and of rejoicing to some. A bird that flies has no barriers. Your globe must have no barriers. The breaking down of structures is very real to you as we speak. You will see more leaders topple, frontiers disappearing and new ones set up. There will be those who are fearful because they know that the structure they live by is a lie and that they are not prepared to make changes. Those who live by their fear will become violent, are violent and aggressive - they will fight with others who have the same fears. They will cause much confusion and hatred because within these individuals all the negative particles that we spoke of before are being drawn together by their own hatred. But they will use up the negative particle energy and once and for all it will be changed to Light.

The Light, the power, the thought energy that fills everything in every part of the Universe is part of you. You are not removed from it. You are a part of it, as are beings from other planets. You are a part of it as we are. Understand you are all part of Light.

Your planet has been a planet of emotion. It has taught other planets much by its struggling and yes, dear children, it has even given the greater Thought, the greater Light some remarkable experiences. By your suffering you have given to the greater Truth and created the opportunity for a greater energy not just for yourselves but for the whole Universe. So we ask you again, at this time particularly, to look within yourselves, to look, to look, to *look*.

II. POINT OF DEPARTURE

You understand the concept of wheels within wheels. Every revolution of a wheel is the completion of a cycle. This is what is happening in your world: you are coming to the end of a cycle. It so happens that it is a small cycle which is inside a larger one, with a larger one outside that, and so on.

To begin with, two inner cycles correspond. There is the cycle of the age that you yourselves measure and live by on your planet, and there is also the ending of a bigger cycle which represents your globe and its relationship to the Universe. Then there is the third cycle of the cosmos, also at its point of change. And so the force, the knowledge, the intuition that every living thing is feeling at this time is much stronger than has perhaps ever before been experienced.

We understand that there is difficulty in interpreting current feelings, some of which are very bold, almost destructive. There is a universal sense of some kind of Armageddon, and even in the least conscious and intuitive individual there is a real awareness of some movement or change. Each individual has to interpret these feelings for himself, but because of the vast, cosmic proportions of the whole change, whatever you think about it cannot alter what is to be.

For some of you there is tremendous responsibility. You need to help break down fears and yet you do not want to impart information that could in itself have a harmful effect on the progress of individuals. Every individual is coming (and in some cases has come) to the level of what you describe as the Christ. This is a reality. More and more individuals will leave their fear behind as they journey to this point.

It is the responsibility of all to listen to the Christ emanation in order to learn what to do and what to say at any given moment. This is not easy even for those who have taken the step of the new consciousness. There will be times when it is difficult and things seem clouded, but these times will be very short. Wait, listen, and equilibrium will return.

You need to know some details of these changes taking place. Every individual already has some knowledge. Unfortunately individuals who are full of fear, knowing within themselves that changes are coming, fight and resist them, giving rise to violence and aggression. It is important at this time to keep calm. Calmness and a stillness within are what will help most.

Many pre-conceived ideas have to break down as individuals rise to the Christ level. There will be a collapse of all kinds of structures within an individual's life. There may be a break-down of the family life, of the work situation, of the home, of all things on the mundane level, and yet the individual can lift himself or herself above all this with increasing ease as the transition progresses.

It will be more difficult for those who have little knowledge and much fear as they see these immense changes occurring for people around them. We are talking about large numbers of people and those who do not rise to the necessary level will see confusion and break-ups and become disoriented. The most negative of these will turn, unfortunately, to violence and crime and to drugs - but you cannot help them. We know this is harsh, but there is little more we can say about it, for the greatest truth is to go with your own spirit.

We talked of the soul. The soul, the spirit within has its own level that connects with, blends with, is part of the Spirit and the Energy beyond the individual. And here is the irony: as you human, living beings break down your outer image, your personality, your ego, to link with the pure energy of the soul, you become less of an individual in the human sense. You will lose your identity, dear children of this beautiful, living, breathing Earth. What you have not fully realised is that you have always been a part of the greater Light, the greater energy. The image, the individuality of the human presence was an important stage to live through. It taught you many, many things. But you never lost and never broke from the higher energy. Yes, dear children, you are indeed a part of the greater Energy that you define as God.

You are therefore now realising your God-potential, or what we describe as the Christ level. It is Christ that you are all aspiring to: a human, living being whom you have accepted as God. This energy will be discussed and confirmed on all levels. It is not just for the psychic and the intuitive: we plainly, firmly say it is for all. For everyone there is a re-shaping of the energy within the individual. The new state will be realised and for some it is even now being realised. It is because the outer image has peeled away that there is or will be a greater concentration of soul energy.

Think on this, dear children, think of the precious, privileged experience of life, the embodiment of the soul energy. As the image breaks away you will find that the individual is more aware of that link to God (we use that word with some reluctance because we know the damage that the image of God has done in your world). Harmony will then be felt with other individuals on that level of being and a kind of group consciousness such as you have never experienced on this planet will come into existence. There will be no more striving and straining to be better than the next person. There will be a kind of love without emotion, but so pure that each individual will know what any other individual requires at any given time. This indeed will be a great communion of souls and so we say in truth that there will indeed be a kind of perfection.

For many, many years people have longed for a society where people truly care for each other. Emotion always distorted this, together with the desire to be better, or to put the ego first. Now you are coming to a time when members of society will truly care and know what the needs of others are, and therefore such things as famine and poverty will not exist. This is your perfect society.

Of course, dear children, you will have some other problems; at each stage, each plateau there is always further to climb. Now you ask what will happen to those who do not move forward to a Christ level. This is not easy for you to comprehend or accept, and we know that even the channeller and her friends will find some of this information difficult. But it is being asked for and we speak in truth.

There will be a polarity of energies. We have already spoken of dark areas and the negative particles within the atmosphere caused by yourselves. At this time there is a real magnetic force in operation. The negative particles are being attracted to certain areas in your globe and the positive ones to others. We know you find this difficult to imagine, but positive and negative will not exist for you in the future - all will be one. We also spoke of people finding their place physically, and that is what is going on now.

There is, and there will be, violence occurring. Imagine a huge magnet which is pulling together all the negative particles and you will see how aggravation and turmoil come about. At this moment there is still an opportunity for individuals in these dark areas to escape. They are not trapped; they can remove themselves if they can let go of their fear. If they choose - and we emphasise, they choose to say - there will be a point of no return for them, because those areas will erupt either through violence and destruction or through what you call natural disaster. The natural disasters will only occur because of negative force in those places. To a large degree the oceans are neither negative nor positive but neutral, although they will be affected to some extent. There will be hurricanes and tidal waves as these energies work out their places, but remember, dear children of God, you cannot save every soul.

So - out of this there is a breakthrough. When the necessary destruction is over, you will be left with just the Light. This will have an enormous effect on every living, breathing aspect of your globe, and even inanimate objects will be affected. The laws of cause and effect or Karma will also go. They are connected to the pulling of energies and the magnetism which is taking place now. There are some who will see only the destruction - that is their choice. There are some so held by their fear that they will cling to people of Light like leeches. There are some who will even try to attack those of Light, not knowing that they cannot be harmed. This is not a question of 'good boys and girls' getting their reward. It is to do with deflection by the energy of the soul and the spirit within.

We must spend some time now on global changes taking place outside your world. We spoke of a cosmic wind. As the energies are changing on your globe, so this is happening on practically every other globe in the whole cosmos. This has already begun. The energy or cosmic wind that is blowing is attracted to globes of higher energy where it is drawn in. This is what is happening on your globe with such powerful result. Other globes which have less energy or are virtually dormant (very few are completely dormant) will be influenced less by the universal wind. This is an incomplete way of describing it but it is one that you can understand.

Everything is balanced, and events in one planet affect every other planet. Your sun is changing, and new energies refreshing old globes will bring about a different physical way of being for you. You see, dear children, the by-products of the Christ consciousness are telepathy, psychic gifts and intuition and everyone will have these. This sensitivity will even enable people to link with souls in other worlds. This is why so many of what you call UFOs are being sighted. As you know, they do not exist physically, but they are there in another kind of reality.

There is a link between peoples of the Universe and very soon in your history there will be, in your words, inter-planetary movement. What you have not realised yet is the great significance of this development. It enables you to free yourself from the burden of the physical - meaning that in reality the spirit inside yourselves goes where it chooses and takes the body with it. There are patterns which govern such movement as it ebbs and flows repeatedly. In your solar system they have been fixed for a very long time, but now new patterns are forming. They are not yet set, and they will not stabilise for some time. This will provide such a freedom of spirit as you have never known and cannot even now comprehend. All we can say is that you will be and are gods.

Your present source of Light, the sun, is going to be conditioned by the winds of change, but it will continue. You will understand the importance of this because you already know scientifically about the energy of your sun. Then one of the other planets in your galaxy will metamorphose to become another source of Light and will position itself close to your globe with the result that there will be no night and day as you now know them. There will be some variance of the Light, but there will be no darkness. You have areas on your globe now which never experience total blackness at certain times of your sun's cycle. It will be similar to that but the cause will be different - the fact that every planet influences the next. When you think about this chain-reaction you can begin to see how even one such change will have enormous repercussions, but we are understating this information because you cannot fully comprehend it at this time, and it is not necessary for you.

The most important aspect of change is and must be for the individual. It is immediate. We do not wish to deprive you of other information, but it can have the effect of distracting the mind from the important issues of this crucial time, when the individual and the individual's growth are paramount Do not think as much of other planets, as of yourselves. Think about your Light and the change of energy within, and these will help you to understand your progression to the next stage.

III. UNDERSTANDING

There is an enormous Breath in the Universe. It breathes out and it breathes in. It has no 'time'.

Time as you understand it is very individual to your own planet. You have measured time from early days through the presence of darkness and Light, your planet revolving around the sun. This measure of time is very personal and individual to you.

We have tried to impart to you knowledge of the essence and the energy within the individual that you call the soul or spirit, which is one with the energy that we have described to you as Thought. It is at one with Thought, but encased in a physical form that you call the body, in order to experience and to grow. But that essence within you has no 'time'. It lives and it breathes as one with the universal Thought to which you are linked. It could be said that the information you are receiving is from you personally, and this would be accurate because all is one. The Thought breathes in and it breathes out.

When your physical body dies, the soul, the spirit takes a journey towards the whole, the Original Thought. The only time when you are able to contact discarnate spirits is when they are in the stage between leaving their physical bodies and being at one with the Source, the Thought. Those soul energies have in the past returned to the world or, as you say, reincarnated to be other individuals with different personalities.

You have been so concerned with outer images that to a large extent discovering what your soul and spirit were in a previous incarnation has not altogether been helpful, some of you heeding only the image and not the essence. For example, you might have been an enormously strong physical warrior in a past life and killed many hundreds of people. In the next life you may have been a tiny, fragile, female person with some physical defect and never had a violent thought in your life. We want to explain to you that the outer image around the encased spirit is not relevant, not important. It merely provides the opportunity for growth and very often in ways you cannot imagine.

Because the original Spirit or Energy is in every part of the whole, time does not exist. We put this to you in terms of human life so that you can begin to understand what we mean when we say, there is no time. We have said to you before that the original Thought has always been there and always will be, and the particles that first separated from it, in order to generate human life as you know it, are still part of that Source. So there is a breathing in and a breathing out of energy that cannot be measured by your time or any time.

Life is an experience within that energy. What you have not understood is that your experiences have altered the energy by bringing back to the Source both growth and experience. There is not one drop more energy than there ever has been. And there is not one drop less. It changes as it expands - a breathing in, a breathing out.

What we are saying is not very easy, and you have asked about "new souls" and "old souls" in relation to timelessness. When you talk of new souls you are talking of an essence or energy that is part of the whole, but has never experienced worldly life before. So it is, in truth, new - new to life. Some souls on leaving life go to what you describe as spirit, then return to a further life. Some souls may not go back always to the Source, but there is always expansion of energy for the soul when it begins as a new soul and then travels forwards. This soul is still part of the whole, the Thought.

We say that some new souls do not go back to the Essence. It is largely to do with attraction. A new soul, as you call it, is particularly involved with the image of life. That experience for that soul is so strong that it comes again and again, because the experiences in life do mould the energy within. But it is not an absolute rule. Sometimes a soul only comes once into life, goes back to the Source and never again returns to life. It largely depends on the experience of living and on a form of attraction that the soul energy creates for itself, which can bounce it back to life or to the Source.

The Thought is conscious. It is aware of itself. The soul, the energy within you is aware of itself. To talk of a soul having a conscious mind is not correct, but the soul is conscious of itself. It is easier for us to speak to you in terms of attraction, and a concept you understand is magnetism, which to some extent explains the moving in and out of the energy. It is an attraction and a growth. But you still put too much importance on the outer image. "I have done well in this life, therefore I will move forward next time". What the individual does in physical terms in his lifetimes may not be what takes him forward to the next. It is realization within the soul. It is the strengthening, the quickening of vibrational essence that allows the person to move forward, and to come from new soul to very old wise soul is not necessarily the purpose of that soul. It is an arrogance on the part of a human to assume that it is.

It is not easy to describe this to you when you continue to value your personality level, even those of you who have largely left the ego behind. The soul is the energy within you that we can see clearly. It is always growing. Growing - not getting larger, but growing in quality. It changes. More simply, it becomes more potent. But we repeat that there has always been the same amount of energy in the whole Universe, the whole Cosmos and that amount of energy will never change. We know that however hard we try to put this in terms you can understand, they are inadequate, only analogies.

The new souls which do not go back to the Source will reincarnate, and a new soul that returns to life usually (but not always) reincarnates in your world again to let the soul have more of that kind of experience. Then later as it moves on, the attraction within its energy becomes such that it can travel back to the Source. There are no more new souls coming in at this time. That is to do with the transition. We do not wish to disturb you, but to a considerable extent the experience of life as you have known it, through your sense of years and time, will never be the same again. The experience that the soul and the energy needed has been achieved; it has been experienced - and it is no longer necessary for more new souls to incarnate.

There has been an enormous quantity of energy on your globe through the souls, the living, breathing things on your planet. Enormous energy, all experiencing life. Again we talk of attraction or magnetism. The energy of your planet has in itself attracted to it at this time what you call old souls. In one sense, dear children, the words 'old' and 'new' are not accurate. Energy is, it was, it always will be. It is a oneness, a completeness, and life is an experience rich with that energy, which has now come largely to its own fulfilment in your world.

We have spoken of physical pain, and how it really does not exist for the soul, the energy within. We will try to put this in simple terms. Think if you can of the energy, the Thought, hard though it is to comprehend. Accept for a moment that it has been there for all time and there really is no beginning, no end. When a magnetic part of that energy separated itself to go on to create numerous worlds, galaxies, stars, and down through that energy your globe, it remained still part of the original whole. And it still has the same amount of energy. As this globe came into being it continued to attract energy to it which became human life. As physical evolution unfolded, taking the Spirit with it, the energy, the spirit, the soul, had an opportunity to expand its level of what we will call consciousness. It was not a case of a purpose, or the deliberate will of some individual or energy. It was simply magnetic attraction.

We have to tell you, dear children, that what you call God is that energy. It is a conscious energy. It thinks, it breathes. It is alive. It is not a personality. And when the essence of the soul comes back to the Source it has no personality or even the remnant of a personality attached to it. But because the experience of all those souls is within that energy, there is with them all knowledge of all times and all people and all living things.

We ask you to think on the Breath. A great breath, breathing in and breathing out. And if you can think of the energy as having its attraction, its magnetism, you may begin to understand how whole universes came to be. But within that energy there is no time. There is experience and there is expansion but no time.

We know this is hard for you. Your scientists will come to this conclusion in their own way. They try to do it through mathematical equations, but without the impetus of the freeing of the imagination they will have limited results. However, the intuition on this globe is heightened now, and will come together with the scientific knowledge. They will in fact be talking of the "breath of life".

You have asked if there are such things as "twin souls". We say with kindness that sometimes people who use this term are not meeting their soul mate but experiencing powerful physical attraction or a number of other things. But when there is a real and true feeling of a deep meeting together, it is very often the case that those two souls have reached the same higher level of energy; they touch and relate to it. And in these cases there is always a feeling of finding God. It is a reflection at a lower level of the feeling and experience that the soul has when it goes back to the Source - connection to the One. It may be that that soul did indeed meet with and experience with the other soul in another lifetime, and so there is a recognition. But it is more likely that the level of the energy within the soul knows its counterpart, knows its unity, feels its attraction, is aware of God. That is why the experience is truly wonderful for the human being. We can talk of feelings of the soul. As we said the energy is conscious. It is not an emotional feeling as you know it, but it is feeling and it is experiencing. We can say that it delights in something - but it is not an emotional delight.

We have to say again, dear children, that you are very privileged. Every living being is privileged to be on this globe, to experience this feeling and growth such as no other living beings have experienced. The magnetism of the energy that brought itself to this globe and used the physical body as an encasement for itself is truly privileged.

In one thing your scientists are correct. There is no other life as you know it in the cosmos. There are other being, breathing, living beings, but none as individual as you. And although the way things have been in the world is coming to an end, and the experiencing of outer image will be dying away, it has been an enrichment for the soul, a growth beyond your present comprehension. And you will go on to evolve, no doubt dear children, to what you call "greater things". The past aeons of suffering have brought immense richness and experience to the energy, the consciousness, to the soul. We know you won't fully comprehend that time does not exist, but for now perhaps it is enough for you just to think of your 'time' as another kind of experience.

You ask to hear of the role of the Masters. Because of evolution there has always been one type of soul that is above or a little bit further along the road of experience than any other. And its soul consciousness does indeed know that it has to come at a particular time to be as a Light to those who can see it. So in a very real way there are teachers. You are approaching a time when that kind of teacher-soul will not be needed.

When we say the words 'needed', 'pleased', or 'feelings' we use human terms, but really we mean magnetism, attraction. But if we were to speak to you in what you would call 'cold' terms, it would not mean very much, and it would not touch your hearts or souls. So we must talk of feelings and needs and pleasures and things of that kind, but they all mean the same.

There are occasions when a certain kind of individual is required. It is again like an attraction, and that soul or part of the energy manifests itself to be a Light, a teacher, but as you are now realising, all knowledge is within because you are all part of God. You belong to God.

Masters and teachers are the awakening ones; they awaken the outer shell and enable the very real touching of the energy within. Groups link together again through this unison, this harmony of feeling the energy.

It all comes back to the original Thought, which is not without its own change. It has changed and expanded in knowledge. It will always expand - but not for great power, for power is only something the image creates. Yes, the Thought is an energy, a force, but not a power for its own sake. It grows but it never gets a minute older.

We understand your dilemma and your questions. You will have to think on these things.

You wish us to speak of your work in contacting discarnate spirits. As souls have progressed, expanded and grown throughout the aeons of your time, most of them are reaching a point where they have no further need for personal images of discarnate spirit. You will be finding that people come to you individually, speaking to you personally and to others for an acknowledgement of their soul-energy growth - a recognition and an acknowledgement. And you will be able to touch them and they will know.

There are indeed discarnate souls which, to simplify it, linger in the outer atmosphere which is an interim stage as they go forward, and before they go back to the Source. They hold with them, are still close to the experience and the personality that they had as a human. Yet again this represents the principle of attraction and magnetism. You and others like you (in fact, everyone) will attract to yourselves those who need and feel they can be helped by you to move forward. This attraction has no limit in distance, but one soul searching for acknowledgement of its growth will be drawn to the nearest living being which is on the level that it recognises intuitively can understand it. So you will find approaching you from your own vicinity those who need and require that kind of response and help.

You cannot think of the concept of timelessness in your own human dimension because of your strong sense of day and night - days, weeks, months, years. But it is all just an experience. No greater perhaps than any other experience of the energy, which is expanding, breathing, growing. It is ever there, ever present, ever growing.

Your scientists are looking at the figure, the equation of 'Z', zero, nothing. Think about that image - nought, nothing, a circle, a round. The energy, the Original Thought, is like that circle. It is always there. It is the Z factor. You are experiencing it now. There is only one Experience and it is all part of the whole. Free your minds. Let go of your outer image. Conquer your fear. The energy of your soul will soar and you will make contact with the Source, with God - and that experience of reunion is beyond your comprehension.

We will now leave you with the thought of the energy, the attraction, the magnetism, and with the image of the Breath, breathing out, going to all living things to experience, and then the breathing in as it comes back with joy and completion.

IV. SOUL ENERGY

We wish at this point to reiterate in simple terms what has been said regarding the energy, to make it more succinct and clear. Every living thing on any living globe has evolved from and is part of the energy that we have described to you as Original Thought. When a human is born, the energy enters into the body. This energy is the life force and without it the body cannot be sustained. Although the biological forces have their own energy, it is inadequate without the life force which is the impetus of all things.

The life force, the soul, settles down within the body. It takes some time for the body to get used to the energy and be at one with it. As we have said, this energy never decreases, ever. It changes, it expands, it grows, but there is no such thing as the soul decreasing or becoming 'bad'. There is no such thing as an evil soul. We repeat that evil has largely developed from the minds and negativity of yourselves. It is difficult for you, still clearly with the image or personality very much in mind, to understand the great synthesis of energy that runs through everything, but it is very real. Everyone living on your globe is in truth a part of all the others, and a part of the whole.

Previously we tried to explain to you the universal breathing in and the breathing out. This is rather a poetical phrase but it does express the reality in a way that you may understand. When the body dies and the soul is released, it returns to the Source as an in breath. When it is born it is breathed out from its origin.

There is a greater reality than you know. You are some way along the road of evolution, and this transition time that you are so interested in is a turning point, where all will begin to understand this togetherness with God. It is not the end of your evolution. There is no end, there is no beginning. It is a oneness, a wholeness, the 'beingness' of a reality.

You are beginning to see the turning of a tide. We speak to you now of the physical, biological aspect. Your body, your planet, have an energy of their own that has certainly evolved from the Original Thought. But this energy, as developed separately and is not, in your terms, the same as the energy of the soul which is, as we have explained, part of the original. The evolution of the physical body and indeed the physical matter of your very globe (and others, but for now we will deal with just your globe) did indeed evolve from the separation or the breathing out from the Original Thought, but it evolved in a specific way: it evolved as physical mass.

Each stone on your planet has its own physical energy. In your body you have a biological energy that has evolved on its own, and you say in your ceremonies that when a body has died, it is "ashes to ashes and dust to dust". This is very apt, because the energy of the biological body goes back into the Earth. It has evolved from the Original Thought, but it has put down its own stamp, its own uniqueness on the result of that process. But we repeat that if there was no soul within the body, you would not exist, you would be like a stone.

Because of the difference in these two energies - the biological energy and the soul energy - there is often conflict between them and that is why babies die, children die, and even why adults die; but where babies accept the synthesis of these two energies, they survive and they grow strong. If, however, there is a rejection of the soul energy, that baby will not survive. The soul of that child will go on and find another home or embodiment for its energy. Nothing is ever lost.

When a baby is conceived there is a magnetism. A soul or energy draws close to the fertilised seed. The soul is very close to the biological growing of the child within the womb, but is not always itself in the womb. It is, as it were, held in a magnetic field near it. Usually at the time of birth the soul enters the baby, the life force breathes out, and this entering-in of the soul becomes the life. Occasionally, because the magnetism is particularly strong, the soul may enter the body of the child before it leaves the womb. It depends on how the magnetism is working between the soul energy and the biological energy. It varies from one instance to another.

The energy that created the child in the womb is largely biological but the mother very often has a strong sense of the baby's soul. She focuses her thoughts within her tummy, and even though that may not be where the soul is at that point, she still feels it. It becomes almost a part of her. You speak of children choosing their parents. This can be said to be true, but it really has to do with the attraction between the energies of the parents and the child.

There are, as you know, deaths in the early days, weeks and months of babies' lives, and although biologically great steps forward have been taken to overcome this, you will never eradicate the death that occurs when the soul and the body fight in the child. In the passing or death of the body there is a separation of the two energies, because the time has come when the soul can no longer expand within that body. After the separation the soul-energy usually goes, as we described before, first to what you describe as 'spirit'. Then, according to its magnetism, it either goes to the Source or comes back to the world again. This is really a re-charging or recycling of energies.

You use the words "as above, so below", and you can see no how people are accepting this idea in actual physical ways. You on your globe are really beginning to understand the value of recycling and how the energy is recycled.

Illness and pain will disappear with this understanding. You find that strange. It is difficult to imagine a time when you cut your finger and feel no pain. But as the body and the soul synthesize in energy, that is how it will be. Illness and disease have only come about through 'bad thought' - in the sense that negative particles in your atmosphere are drawn in to an individual who accepts them and becomes physically ill as a result.

We ask you to think. We give you a description, an analogy of the energies. You have a clear bottle of water. Put some oil into it and you will see the oil separate out into little globules. The globules will come together and patterns will be formed. No matter how much you shake the bottle, not one drop of that oil disappears. That is how the energy is. It never disappears.

Many people will be interested in our words because they want information about how this transition in your time is taking place, or rather what disasters may happen. We find it unhealthy to make this kind of detail known generally. At this time you must learn to rise above your negativities and we will do nothing to enhance them, although there is other information for those who can truly and rightly accept it. Regarding disasters, however, there will be some clearing away by this method, but remember, dear children, no energy disappears. Nothing is wasted. And even in disasters, wars and famine, energy of the soul goes on, lives on, breathes on. The ordinary human identity is lost, but the identity at this time is being removed in any case. Even the starchy, rigid minds of men have noticed and are feeling what we describe to you as the 'wind of change'. It is a joy. It is a time of illumination. A freeing time. An expanding time.

The most important aim of these words coming through your 'channeller' is to convince the individual to look within himself instead of outside himself. We want people to look within, to catch hold of this wind of change and dispel the negativities from themselves - so that they may soar to the sky. That is what is important.

You are receiving help. Your globe is receiving help. We spoke to you before of some intervening energies beyond your own which are hovering around your globe. Do not be concerned for you have a ring of protection around you and your globe will not be destroyed. We say this with absolute certainty, from direct knowledge. Your globe will not be destroyed until it has evolved to a point where it has no meaning. But that is not now. The protection is in the form of energy. There are some beings from other globes who are drawing close to you. They are watchers and helpers and they are fascinated by you. We remind you yet again of the uniqueness of the human state.

The time will very soon come when your need of these helpers is great and they will make contact in a very real, practical way. Already preparations are being made in people's consciousness to help them accept this, and it is happening through your images, your media. But the largest part of this transition must and will come from individual growth. The beings and the energy outside your globe are like mothers watching their children take their first steps on their own.

It is disappointing that you have created so many negative particles around your globe, and these have to be dissolved. They will be drawn to special areas with the help of the energy above your globe and of all the higher beings on your globe. They will dissolve once and for all, these negative particles that have created so many problems for you.

A negative particle released into the atmosphere should dissolve itself in the Light of truth. But over your aeons of time they have accumulated and have become very dense on your globe. Yet there have always been higher souls and sometimes energies from other globes to help dissipate the negativity. You can imagine the difficulty they had, and you owe them much, for there have been periods when the negativity was like a dark, impenetrable cloud and your globe and the people on it might have disappeared forever in it.

Now Light is coming; in fact, Light is here, and some of you really feel this. When the crystal-like negative particles in the atmosphere are exposed to the Light they will reflect Light and so lose their negativity, which will dissolve. That is what is happening, and you are able to watch it day by day which is exciting for you. It is a joy.

Those of you who have overcome the level of negativity must and will keep up the work of radiating Light around you, and this will help others near you to do the same for others near them and so on. It is like spreading an infection, an infection of Light, and in even the darkest corner, the tiniest candle is a signpost pointing forward. Be vigilant. Be strong.

It is important for you to understand the energies and how they work. You understand how electricity is formed; sometimes from fuel, sometimes from water and even from the sun. They are different levels of energies working in their own way but they all have the same end result - that when you flick the switch, as it were, your light bulb glows. We will call you warriors of Light, but there is no fighting involved. There is an acceptance and a rising to a higher level.

We know that you feel pity and sympathy from the pictures which reach you of people in places far from you who are in pain and suffering. You want to help. Dear children, you can help by this infusion of Light within yourselves. You see, there truly is no such thing as an evil soul. An individual can be evil only in the sense that he has taken into himself all the negative energy which then surrounds and masks the soul. But the soul and its energy are still there. The Light is still there. Negative minds and thoughts cause destruction of some individuals and particularly of groups of individuals who have attracted negativity. If you are perceptive you can recognise this negative attraction. That you can describe as evil, but a soul is not evil. A soul just is.

If a soul has been wrapped up in darkness in a particular life it obviously does not grow in that life. That means it has not progressed, and the strength of the personality or image goes with the soul in its interim stage of spirit and then the soul is reborn. Hitler, perhaps currently the epitome of evil to you, is an example of that circumstance.

Hitler died a violent death. He lived in darkness and he was wrapped in a mind which delighted in negative energy. He found a strength in that energy and its image was immense to him. He was all the things you know of him - arrogant, conceited, domineering - all those things and yet his soul was Light. His soul had been trapped until it was released by his violent death. It had not been allowed to grow so it was stunted. It went into spirit and it was (in terms you may understand) 'looked after' there. But it could not go back to the Source because its energy, its magnetism, had not expanded to allow it to do so.

Gradually and with help Hitler's image-personality, so strong within the knowledge of the soul, in spirit, will to some extent be dissipated. His soul has indeed been reincarnated; we can tell you this. When it was prepared (we ask you to understand that that word is not exactly what is meant, but must serve) - when it was prepared in spirit to go back to your globe it had realization of an opportunity for growth. In fact, that soul is a child at the moment. It will not have any of its previous personality. It will be an ordinary child living out difficult situations, but with a loving mother and some comfort from the father to enable the soul to grow. This surprises you. You feel that the destruction he caused previously should be punished. It is punishment enough not being allowed to expand.

Sometimes evil people, individuals who have attracted negativity within themselves, are very ordinary when they return to the world. The soul pays by its limited, stunted growth. Imagine for a moment you are little children, girls and boys who have to live in an iron box, in darkness with no Light whatever. You would not grow strong. This is how the soul is stunted.

There is not, and never has been, such a thing as retribution as you understand it. Negative energy attracts negative energy. The soul of Hitler is now a child in South America in a poor family. A sickly child, physically sickly, a child not starving but often hungry. The mother loves the child. Because the soul has been used to darkness there is a danger, and it does often happen, that the soul then attracts more darkness to it in a further lifetime, and that is what you call Karma, the law of Cause and Effect. The child with the soul of Hitler will never be known to the world. Now it has an opportunity for growth. It must shake off once and for all its acceptance of darkness around it.

You ask about the balance of Light and darkness in yourselves, and whether the shadowy side of you will now be eliminated. As you understand it the answer is quite simply yes. We have tried to convey to you the reality of the great energy that holds within itself the energy of the soul. It contains no darkness. There has been a strange balance on your globe of Light and dark, caused originally by the early people's sense of night and day, but there is no real darkness in the world. It is not so much that it is disappearing, but more that there is now knowledge that it never really existed.

You want to know what the energy was, known as the Devil, which tempted Christ in the wilderness. You must remember that this truly elevated soul, Christ, had to deal with all the ordinary things of the human condition. He was perhaps the strongest realization in human form up until that point, of God in Man. But, dear children, he was not perfect. He was an evolved man. That particular incident was not so much the experience of temptation for him as it was the acknowledgement of the darkness - the dark particles, the negativity - and his final and irrevocable knowing that he could have no part in it. It was not a question of temptation from a man with a horned head, your concept of the devil. That image is just a personification of the negative particles we speak of. It is easier for some to give them personified form, but it is not so.

Christ wanted that test. He even attracted it to him, and he came out of it with an expanded soul - even the soul of Christ grew in his own lifetime. You speak of him dying on the cross for mankind, and he died on the cross because his image or personality was so strong that it offered an opportunity for the rejection of darkness, transforming it into Light, which is to say that the personality has to die to bring in the Light.

The image of Christ dying in pain and in suffering for the world has inspired and given courage to some people to pursue their evolution. But now at this time you have the opportunity to be your own Christ.

V. EXPANSION

Instead of it receding, as it needs to now, there is growing fear among the peoples of the world. There have already been some extraordinary events at the beginning of the time of change and people can see for themselves that something very unusual is happening. There is also a growing number of people who cannot cope with the new energies coming in; and they are affected both mentally and emotionally, and your clinics and your hospitals will be kept busy. Some people who are becoming fearful do not even want to go outside their own front door. They will even go without the necessities of their daily life to avoid it. In this year 1990 there will be freak weather conditions, for instance. Already there have been earthquakes, rains, winds, high waves; water flowing where it normally does not go.

Although there won't be a common consensus that something radical is happening, within the majority of life forms there will be a true sensing of it. There is a stimulation being applied to all people, in all countries. The words we convey are given specifically for this time. What can people do? As we have said, there will be some who cannot be helped, who cannot let go of their negativities because the energy of their souls is too weak; there are some who understand, are unafraid and move forward in Light; and in between there are those who are hesitant, concerned, even worried , but fortunately have not been taken over by panic. There are different ways for different people, and it is up to the middle section of individuals to expand the energy of their own souls to dissipate their negativity. Most of all they need to learn to find their silence, their stillness within. A form of meditation can be of enormous help. They cannot push their negativity away, neither can they ignore or hide it.

Stimulation of the energy of the soul at this time will cause it to radiate strength and Light and to dissipate the negative particles or crystals on the different human levels - particularly the mind. We ask all to identify with, to touch, to breathe the stillness and the Light - and to trust; to trust not so much God as the God-within-themselves, because this is what the transition time is for. That is what Christ-consciousness is about: God in human form. It is time to acknowledge and fully realize at last that you yourselves are God and that the energy of your soul is a synthesis of what you can call the God-Source.

Whenever there is worry or fear we suggest that you sit down, quieten your mind, concentrate on the Light, the energy, the stillness within and with every breath concentrate on expanding that Light. This is very easily done once there is acceptance of needing to do these things. They represent quite simply the energy of the soul expanding readily and smoothly, and this will in itself clear negativities.

We ask everyone to look at their worst fears and know that they can pass through them and beyond them so that nothing will ever be 'bad' for the individual again. We are aware that most of you are frightened of death and pain, but much knowledge has accumulated down through the ages about cleaning away the fear of death. Your soul, your spirit lives on. The body, the image, is only an illusion. Pain is a more difficult consideration. No one wants pain and nobody truly wants others to be afflicted by it. As the stimulated energy in you grows, it does so in such a way as to dispel the illusion of the body, the image. After that the body will work with better harmony and diseases will no longer be caught or contracted. Illnesses will not be attracted to those of higher energy, and so pain will disappear from your world.

Those who can reach this higher level will come to a point when even confronted by someone with a knife about to kill them, they would feel no fear - although in reality the level of energy that emanates from a 'higher' individual would probably preclude such an occurrence.

We have spoken of the marked difference that you will see during the next months and years between those who rise in energy and those who do not. People who are 'left behind' are like sediment at the bottom of the sea while others rising to the top breathe in the atmosphere of new Light, new hope, new radiance. So, dear children, deal with your fear. Fear is the main reason we are talking to you.

As time goes on there will be more and more 'channellers' of information from beyond your world. Eventually all will be able to channel their own information. We ask you to visualise a six-pointed star made up of two triangles, one of them inverted, laid one on top of the other. See yourself standing in the space at its centre, with the top point of the star linking you to the Source and the base line of that triangle across your body just above your solar plexus. Think of a strong flow of information, energy and Light coming down to you from above. Those who have dispelled fear will be able to do this and obtain their own channelling information. This is not a select, elitist procedure - it is open to all.

Within the two triangles of that star, there is a synthesis of the energy from you, the individual, and from the Original Thought. There will be some difference in the approach and style of information channelled, and this is to do with the individual concerned, but the foundation of all knowledge sought and derived in this way will be reliable. Of course, channelling is not something new. There have been channellers on your globe for many aeons, but what is new is that those who move forward into what you call the New Age will all be able to 'tune in' to perfect Truth. There will be an overall attunement.

We ourselves can see clearly the level of the energy within each individual. We are able to watch it expand and grow, and it is a delight to us.

The energy of those who have expanded their Light joins with (and will join with) the energy that is being attracted to your globe. We spoke earlier of an intervening force at this time. This is deliberate, positive intervention to do with higher energies being attracted to it, similar energies some of which come from Original Thought. Some comes from other beings of life energy on other globes. There has been a recognition of these other beings, a very real acknowledgement. Their energies and our energy hover together until the magnetism or attraction between them has reached such a degree that they can combine in a new, balanced form - much as the comprehensive shape of the six-pointed star emerged from the two separate triangles. The combining of the forces is a synthesis. This new energy will flow round your globe as a kind of healing, a dispelling energy.

You cannot yet imagine what your globe will be like in the future, you who have lived through many generations, your lives cloaked by negative particles. Your globe will be free of them, and it will be Light. There will therefore be a kind of perfection. Your grass will still be green, your trees will still have leaves, you will still have animals and other living things, but some species will disappear and others will evolve further.

This does not mean that your globe will cease to progress. There is never an end to evolution and growth. But in very real ways this time sees the beginning of what you would call paradise. We give you an image of a globe covered in Light with lush grass, trees without diseases, people without diseases. Some of those who are in conflict within themselves would readily admit that that kind of world would not suit them.

We spoke before of the man called Hitler and we tried to explain to you how his positive energies were overwhelmed. He enjoyed his negativity; he gained power from it. There are those today who like to gain power and would hate not to command that negative force. They are people who cannot, will not expand their soul and they will therefore not live again in this world.

We have spoken of an 'infection' of energies. When the expansion gets going, it will gain momentum so fast that some of you will not be able to keep pace with it. But as the momentum increases more and more souls will expand. The more souls that expand, the more souls CAN expand. The infection is really an infusion of energy. There are souls in what you call spirit which understand very well what is happening. Some of these elevated souls are working with various individuals to guide them. You speak yourself of 'guides' and it is true that there are guides to help. But we must say, with some

52

reluctance, that there will be a time after this transition when there will not be a separate place of spirit. The place of spirit in itself is a temporary 'home' that will eventually no longer be necessary.

The human image, the ego, is disappearing. It will not live on. But we repeat that all experiences are taken into and held in the soul, like a programme in a computer. No experience is ever lost to the soul, but the image or identity that lived it is dissolving fast. Then there will be no need to link with guides or those in spirit. Indeed there will not be any elevated souls in spirit because by that time when death occurs the soul will most likely go straight to the Source. Death of the body will in any case be less frequent then because of the new strength; we are speaking of a time something like ten, fifteen or twenty years ahead. People who go forward into that time will sing together in harmony, will sway together, will *be* together.

Men have cherished ideals of united countries, a united world: Utopia. They have tried to achieve it through the inadequate means of governments and policies and politics. It never worked then because of the temptation of the ego, but we tell you that soon you really will have your perfect community.

Eventually there will be no need for electrical communication of any kind. Why pick up an external instrument when you have a superior one within you by which to communicate with others? There will be no need for mechanical vehicles either. Why climb into a cumbersome vehicle when you can be anywhere you want in a moment without it? And there will be no need for metal birds in the sky because you will all be able to fly. You may think this is just poetic imagination on our part, but we tell you that it is real.

Those of you who expand in Light will notice how fit you become. You will have no illness or disease, and if needed your bodies will repair themselves. This is because of the energy.

You speak of good, and God. There will be come people who look upon you as 'expanded' ones as the devil incarnate, or as some trick of the Light or the devil. But no devil exists. You have angels around you, angels of Light in these momentous times. With the freeing of the heavy force as it sinks and dissolves within the sea of Light, you will soar to higher things.

You speak of love. The love that without human emotion is so pure and beautiful, so great that it is beyond your perception. And although you will not truly experience the total beauty of this love until you have evolved even further than we have described, you will in due course begin to see a reflection of that love.

You speak of caring for others, and there are many who do care for others, but of those do so for their own reasons, their own selfish purpose. That is not love. We tell you that after the transition you will all automatically care for others because you will know that others are a part of you.

You speak of twin souls, the feeling of God-connection when two souls of the same higher energy meet. We tell you now that this is what you will all experience - a meeting of souls.

Watch out for animals. Dogs are particularly susceptible to the currents of negativity and fear, so be careful of them for they will become more aggressive. Those of you who expand your energy need not fear the bites of dogs. Your energy itself will deflect the aggression. You will see some dogs go mad. Let the animals which have chosen extinction die as they will. Do not intrude on them with injections or drugs. Their time will be over and their work done.

The land masses will change and different maps will have to be drawn up, but we spoke of a constant level of energy in the whole cosmos and there will be almost the same proportion of land to sea on your globe then as there is today. No energy is ever destroyed, it merely changes, and as you now know you are seeing a change of energy at this time.

Dear children, you have within yourselves the potential to grow the perfect Light, and yet you have done great wrong to your animals. Look at the elephants, for instance; they are feeling it and they are crying out. But do not be afraid, you have also given them strength. There is God in all living things.

Dear children, you will have no need of government; there will truly be government by the people. There will be unity. We can tell you clearly that there will be no leaders. All will lead and all will serve.

We have already spoken of a change in the climate which will remove some of the reason for living in a dwelling. But you will still have homes of a sort, although the shape and size may be different. There will be no criminals so you will have no need of locks or keys. Because the climate is more temperate, there will be no need to shut your windows. This change will come about gradually as your needs alter. The gradual changes to the dwelling-lace of which we speak will come about after the transition time.

Just imagine what can be accomplished within the freedom of perfect harmony. There will be no stagnation, only growth. And it will be your growth, in your way, in your time.

Children go to school now to learn to read, to write, and they will still learn those things then. Writing will still be needed, but there are many other things that children learn now at school which will no longer be necessary, and so they will eventually not be taught. When a baby learns to feed himself you do not have to teach him how, because he already knows. That is how it will be then. Do not be afraid or fear the changes; they are dramatic, but when things become redundant they will disappear as a natural course of events. Children will be taught by their parents, by those around them and by the school of life. Remember that your children will be more evolved and stronger than you are today, and everyone will live longer.

We have to speak now of the transition time itself. By making specific dates known to others you may do more harm than good, but we will tell you that by the year 2001 you will see and experience something of the New Age that we have described to some extent. The breaking down and sinking of the heaviness of negativity and fear will accelerate from next year onwards; particular dates are neither relevant nor important to know. It will all happen like a falling stone accelerating down a cliff, and to say that the stone will be in one place at one particular moment in time is futile. If we were to give you specific dates you might concentrate your negativity and actually destroy your opportunity for growth. You will have to attune yourself in order to know what to do.

Take one step at a time and with each step you will expand. And as each step becomes smoother, easier, eventually you will run free with no pain, no suffering, no effort.

VI. DISCRIMINATION

You people of the Earth have long needed and wanted to personify everything. You speak of God as a person, you speak of the devil as a person. Any negative force which is attracted to an individual or a place is perceived on your inner levels as darkness and coldness and fear come from it. It is then sometimes pictured in the mind in a human form as a horrid monster, cruel and evil.

There is danger here. Think of negative particles in the atmosphere as a cloud, which changes its form and can be shaped into evil figures. When the negative energies are perceived in this way, they are given a life of their own. This has happened often. People have even consciously used the negative crystals to create their own monster with humanoid form, and given it a name. Such a being has an energy of its own which is negative, but it cannot live on its own. It can only subsist on the negative thought of and negative attraction to the individual who originated it. It is, however, a creature which can function and it does evil work for the originator who 'feeds' it.

So here is the dilemma. There is an entity made of evil which does not live and breathe in the same way as you, yet does exist and has power. Usually when the individual who created it (either consciously or through their own fear) dies, or else banishes it, the entity will dissolve. But some evil entities are so strongly formed that they have carried on from generation to generation.

Your name for people who deliberately create these negative beings is "magician". Some, very few, realize just what they are doing.

A similar pattern occurs for people who don't consciously create beings but who let in negative force at a particular time and involuntarily create within themselves a negative feeling powerful enough to become an entity. Such intended beings have done much harm, and the alliance between them and the individuals who originated them is always an unhappy one. But just as we have described how negative crystals can be dissolved through Light, so these entities can also be broken up into separate particles and dissolved in Light.

There was one particular stage in your history when fear - caused by narrowness of mind, bigotry, resentment and an urge-for-power - was so great that negative-force beings were rife on your globe. But Light prevailed. We repeat to you that only out of negativity within the individual can such beings arise, and now at this time they are less common, although they do still exist.

We have spoken much of fear and the great necessity at this time to dispel it. We ask you to think about what we have told you and understand just how dangerous and destructive negative 'monsters' can be once they have been created. But remember, dear children, they are only created from negativity and from fear.

Personifications have also been created out of Light, though in a different way. Because of your desire for perfect beings, saints or messiahs, you have projected thoughts of perfection, Light and truth onto certain individuals (usually 'dead') whom you have assumed or felt were made of goodness (and most of them were).

In this way the energy of Light was directed to actual individuals. However, because the urge to personify good has been so powerful, it has become a desire to connect to nothings less than gods, and human energy has created many god-like figures out of ordinary, good individuals.

You have put a heavy burden on those souls, most of whom are 'dead', and as a result of your thoughts and desires, however positive, they have not been allowed to move on. They have been willing to accept this, in order to guide and comfort you, but it is time now, dear children, to stop looking outside yourselves for gods or for devils. You must and you will look within. How else, dear children can you move on?

Yet again, it is a question of energy. Imagine for a moment how much energy has been poured out towards saints and gods of many names. Think for a moment how many prayers have been said in the Christian faith, particularly to Christ and the woman you call Our Lady. Consider how much energy has gone into deifying them and the saints. Because they were truly elevated beings they have given themselves to service and would continue to do so if it were healthy and wise quite willingly, without any grudge, regret or bitterness - but they know and we know that that time has come to an end.

We have spoken of intervention. We intervene to clear away or neutralise negative energies. We are peeling them away from you. It is as though we are taking away the skin because the goodness of the fruit is hidden beneath it - but it is happening within the individual. This is our intervention, and it cannot be done for everyone en masse, like the waving of a magic wand. It must be done individually. There is a raising and an expansion of energy of the soul that reaches a point where the need for external gods is no more.

There are many things that stop the soul's expansion and the greatest of them is fear. But, dear children, once you turn your thoughts to the whole concept and reality of the energies - how they move, how they attract, where they come from and where they go - and know how to co-operate in them, then it becomes very easy. There have always been currents of energies, whether they have been realised or not. In the past you have given them different names. Among them you have named your devils and you have named your gods. Now we are taking the names from you because the energy has no name. It just is.

Other beings on your globe have also been affected by this pattern. All living things are being influenced. You find it strange to talk of rocks and stones as living things, but they are and they are being affected. If you turn up the temperature under a cooking pot it will boil and blow the top off. This is what can and will occur in all your structures - a moving and shifting with the change of energy; but do not be afraid for it is in fact a natural progression, even though we talk of intervention. Your globe is like a pot being stirred. As the energy rises there is a form of boiling taking place. It is a disturbance, but you so often think of disturbance as negative. This is a positive disturbance shifting, moving, pushing all living things.

It is even in every single grain of your soil. Walk into a forest, stand still and link yourself to the earth's energy. You can feel it - through the soles of your feet and through the trees. There are creatures and plants in the Earth. You can feel the energy and the life in your Earth, and just as some of you are really perceiving within yourselves the change and the heightened energy, so it is with the Earth. It is changing and shifting. Soil will move; rocks will move; trees will move. Your climates will move. But this shift or disturbance is not an evil one.

We blow the wind of new energy towards you, the breath of new energy. It has already begun. And there will only be a short space of time before this breath of energy is no longer directed to you. It is meant to start you flying, to allow you to take off, and as you take wing, you will fly on your own.

Some of you are interested in other globes and beings. There are other beings on different globes who know of the wind of change that is blowing. On some globes it has already affected part of their particular evolution, so they have completed their change and the wind has left. We point out again how interested other beings are in your globe as what you would call a "test case", and most of them know that all energy is within all living things, and part of a unified power. They also know their connection to you, and some of you are discovering your connections to them.

Unfortunately, because of your tremendous desire for personifying and 'naming', some of you have placed this thought/energy of your 'gods' and 'devils' on to the beings from other globes. These beings find it strange, but they are curious about the thought and the energies you send towards them. So they have drawn towards you and some of them are in touch with you in much the same way as we are speaking to you now. Learn from them, but we ask you not to make them your new gods. Their mind has been stimulated and they want to discover.

Some people would readily pull these beings apart in trying to understand them. Dear children, you have been pulling your gods apart for too long. Learn what you can: acknowledge them and open your minds to the curiosity and knowledge they can bring. Do not carve them into little pieces and again create negative entities. We do not want to see that situation, because your gods must be dissolved. Your desire is so strong that you could merely transfer your desires from one name to another. *There are no new gods.*

The beings from other globes are different from you. Many of them (and particularly those that some of you are in contact with), are truly beings of Light. They have evolved, but they have not necessarily gone through the same evolution as you. As already stated, you are unique. One tiny change in the chain of evolution makes an enormous difference.

When these beings are in touch with you, some of them can come inside your being. The first thing they are aware of is your lack of energy in the brain. Your mind has less than one-sixth of their energy. They are puzzled. "How are these Earth beings able to do anything with so little activity of the mind?".

Then they feel your physical strength and there is some concern, for they are not physical in the sense that you are. They are aware of your physical strength and they have no fear, not in the way that you have, but there is a concern. It is rather like you imagining yourself to be a dinosaur with the strength and power that those creatures had.

Then they are aware of your emotions. They are disturbed by these and they do not understand. They have nothing to use as a guide to the emotions, because it is one aspect of life that they have never had to deal with.

They breathe in through Light. They do not have organs as you understand them. They have tremendous perception of brain activity, and they can perceive through the level of the brain activity the things that you perceive in physical form; they can 'translate' them, but the emotions they do not understand. We are describing to you now one kind of being. It is a kind you are most in touch with because of the close attraction of your energies. *You* are beginning to breathe in Light, and they are beings of Light, and they are interested and it is through their attraction of like-to-like that they have made contact with you.

They mean you no harm whatever, but they do not understand you. They do not know love as the emotional love you know. They know necessity and they know caring. There is a learning process here for them and for you, and although they have not yet reached its conclusion, they will discover that in many ways you are greater than them. They are at the turning point of developing not their emotions, but their love. You are at the turning point of rising above the lower emotions to the higher levels of pure love, and so you will meet with them and there will be a fusion of energies.

You have asked if they will live amongst you, but because of the very great difference in the way they breathe and their life force, this cannot be, not as a constant state - but they can be with you as a spirit and a soul. You have found now, dear children, your long lost cousins, and they have found you. We do not name them, but they are here and they are real.

Through their curiosity and their being, made largely of what we can only describe to you as Light or spirit, they have the capacity to get inside you. When this happens you call them "walk-ins". It happens because of the attraction, which may be and often is completely unconscious to the individual concerned. These walk-ins are extremely rare. They occur because of a kind of curiosity or specific attraction.

By some of these different examples, you now have knowledge of the reality which is transpiring. It is a chain reaction throughout the Universe, affecting every living thing, every bit of energy, but in different ways.

VII. AWAKENING PERCEPTION

We come to you in harmony and unity. We have been trying to impart to you the reality of energies, of magnetism - and to emphasize that the changes of this time are about the stimulation of energies within the individual. There has always been magnetism between living life forces and it has worked on different levels. There is one type of attraction at the individual soul level but there is another at the level of the mind.

Mind energy works rather like electrical impulses, which is an idea familiar to you. Your mind constantly sends out a pattern of electrical charges - a frequency. It has long been known that the thought and the will of an individual create for him his own reality, and it is used by him for overcoming obstacles, as well as physical illness and disease. The whole question of energy of the mind is now of paramount importance, since the mind affects every facet of the individual.

The soul functions something like a battery within you. A soul that is clear and unblocked permits greater brain facility, provides a strengthening of the spiritual body and the pure love beyond emotion.

We will have to use analogies now which are somewhat inadequate, but we think will give you a sense of what we mean. If your battery (your soul) is covered over, it cannot release its charge and the current cannot flow properly. Every individual has a slightly different level of energy which is unique to the individual. There are some souls with a very low level of energy, so that the darkness and negativity around them is able to envelop these easily. We spoke of this earlier when we spoke of the man Hitler. The majority of people no longer have a low energy of soul: they have an expanded soul.

At this time, with the stimulation going on from outside which we have described, the energy of the soul or 'battery' is very highly charged. This in turn is sending impulses to the body and to the brain. The brain, the mind is uncharted land for you. None of you readily understands how the energy of the brain functions, but now there will be a big step forward for you because of the higher frequency of the soul energy. It is charging forwards and upwards into the mind, opening up doors that have never been opened. When you walk into an empty room in a new house, you have to fill it. Some of these rooms which have been opened now need to be filled. They need to and must be filled with a clarity and a lightness. At the moment most of you have only got as far as putting light bulbs in the sockets in your new rooms.

All this is a whole new approach for you. For some the sudden change of energy is so great that they cannot stand it, because the energy that the mind emits is powerful. You can speak of it as the sound, the transmitter, the speaker of the soul. This charged energy is also affecting other areas of the brain which already have their doors open, so there may be reactions that you cannot understand.

There is a new perception for sight. Individuals are physically seeing differently. Sometimes this accelerated energy gives them pictures so sharp, so Light that they can hardly bear to look. They are seeing reality with an artist's eyes. This enhanced sight will gradually bring about a change where the individual will be able to see inside things physically: the veins of trees, the skeletons, the bones. This has already happened to certain people. Those who experience it may at first feel they must be going mad, but they are not. They may not be believed, they may be treated as cranks or frauds, but they are not mad.

The accelerated energy is affecting the hearing too. Human hearing is beginning to receive frequencies and sounds much higher than its usual pitch. This is leading to a jangling of sound, so that in crowded rooms where there are lots of voices and sounds, people cannot cope with it because they are beginning to hear everything. They can even hear the sound of the leaves growing on the trees.

All the senses are altered. The perception of taste is sharpened: it is like a blind man suddenly seeing Light, and it is dazzling. Smell is similarly affected. In some cases the effect is so strong that there may be a blocking out of these senses. When a blind man suddenly sees, he cannot tolerate it for great lengths of time; in between he will keep his eyes closed, or wear dark glasses. So in some cases there may be a sudden disappearance of a sense of smell, or taste, or sight, or hearing. In most cases this will only be temporary until the body adjusts to its new frequency.

Once the rate of frequency is raised it cannot be lowered again. There is no such thing as energy dying. Once this battery is charged it does not deplete, it does not go flat. So the stimulation of energies at this time is permanent. We emphasize that the stimulation is not just because of our intervention in your world. It is a combination of intervention and the raising of what is already there. We are merely stoking the fire. The fire already exists and it burns brighter after a little disturbance of the embers.

We cannot emphasize enough how important it is for the individual to understand and accept the new, raised energy on his own level of being. There must be no desire to cling on to, or lean on, what you have called gods. There are higher and lower energies within living beings. Some of you comprehend that, others do not. But this does not mean that those who do not, or only very little, can lean on those who do. There can of course be words of comfort given, reassurance from one to another out of compassion and love. But there must be no dependency, and those of you who have accepted the higher energy must not allow it. Dependency can cloak the soul once more and stunt its growth, or it will badly confuse the mind.

The new stimulation and raising of energy also affects the magnetic frequency in the body, the flow of blood and the cells, and this brings strength, dear children. We have told you that there will come a time when there is no more pain or disease. When the stimulation declines and the body, mind and the soul really work together, the cells, the whole physical state of the body will be stronger. Cells will work more effectively; your blood will no longer cause clots or heart disorders. Such illness or disease as there is will be minimal compared to present levels. Your blood stream is already very much affected, and just as the change in your senses can overwhelm and 'block off', so too the physical level changes will sometimes be too powerful and 'cut out'. For some, change of the cells within the body will unfortunately mean more blood disorders, but only for a time.

The sun gives you Light; in fact it gives you life, but if you were to stand in the hot desert sun for even a short period of time, it would kill you. That is how it is with the incoming energy. It is a strength, a life force, but it also belongs to the individual. We reiterate that the approaching developments are nothing to do with your goodness or your evil. It is all part of the great change in the whole Universe. But, dear children, because you have already raised the level of your energy, it can all come about without catastrophe, although there will be some casualties. That is why we continually emphasize the importance to you, dear children, of acknowledging this 'raising up' - and your own ability to go with it.

From the turn of the century you have been interested in the mind, the psychological aspect of man. This was the foundation of your self-awareness. That whole new perspective on humanity permitted the individual to see himself, become illuminated by self-knowledge - and the new generation is now aware. Evolution always moves on. Each new generation has a new 'rainfall', a new quality. There are always some who are more knowledgeable or 'higher'. There are always some who get left behind. But in every generation there is opportunity for growth.

You have reached a point now where your own energies, strengthened over generations, can truly reach a higher level. The energy of the mind, which comes from the battery of the soul, is making electrical currents in the atmosphere. It really is charging the atmosphere.

We have spoken much of magnetism and the emanation from the individual that stems from the soul, but there is also the speaker of the soul: the mind, which emits its own sound and frequency. This can be both disturbing and tranquil, depending on the energy level of the individual, and be sure of this, dear children: you all perceive these energies. There is often a drawing away of the lower energies from the higher - they cannot stand it. Nor can they bear negative-energy disturbance in the outer atmosphere. These negativities are not just in the outer atmosphere but have crept into what you would call 'the astral'. This must not continue. But now with the wind of change blowing the negativities are dissolving and you stand free of them, on your own. You must learn a new independence of soul and spirit. There is no darkness, only Light, dear children, and you, the ones who expand, will know this to be true.

We talk to you as the conscious, living, breathing energy that we are. We have spoken through others in the past and because at that time the human need was so strong for a personality or identity, we represented ourselves as an identity, or we worked through a spirit that had an identity. But there will be an end of the need for talking to a personality on your part. More and more you will not have to talk with us through a third party. You will talk directly to us. Remember, we are part of you and you are part of us. Dear children, you can talk directly to God, and we ask you to look. Can you not see? Can you not open your mind to the reality that the energy within all living things comes from the same Source - and that you yourselves have done damage between living things. You have done damage to us all.

However, we of the Source are undamaged because of the higher energy, and therefore it is not possible for souls to join us which are not of the same high frequency. But from the Source you came and to the Source you will one day return.

If you think a negative thought towards your brothers and sisters, you send that thought back to yourself, because you are all one. Thoughts are speakers of the soul. If you harm another soul you hurt or harm yourself.

Watch your flowers grow. Rejoice and look at them with your new perspective of the higher energies. Watch them. See their heightened colours and hear the sounds that they make pushing up out of the soil, expanding and coming into bloom, opening out; and know, dear children, that this is what is happening to you too.

You want to know if we come to you from another dimension, but it is not a question of dimension as you perceive it. Let us say this: there are sounds beyond your hearing. You know this. You know that creatures on the Earth perceive sounds you humans cannot hear. In simple terms we are on a different frequency from you - but now you have opened to it. It is a frequency rather than a dimension, and one that up until this time very few of you could perceive.

You measure your world, and we know what you mean when you speak of different levels of consciousness and enlightenment. You are right, dear children, but it is both simpler and more difficult to understand. We will speak simply. As the level of your soul expands, so does the level of your consciousness. You can indeed speak of this progress as steps or stages, but it is better seen as a flow in which there is a point where the petals of a new awareness unfold. It is a trigger point.

There are innumerable levels of growth and your esoteric teachings have spoken of them. You can rightly say we are on the highest level, but do not measure yourselves for this will restrict you. Better, dear children, to know that your energy cannot be destroyed and that you are always moving forwards, and one day you will reach the stage where your soul-energy is such that it is drawn back to its true, original home.

We spoke earlier of the Original Thought, the Energy, Purity. That is what your channeller is in touch with today and what others are reaching and will reach. It is easier sometimes for us to speak of levels as you comprehend them; they are not exactly erroneous, but we should say that they may limit you. You can however sail through, expand and reach up to the highest Light if you know first that you can.

The heightening of energies is allowing you to take an enormous step in evolution, because you will be comparable to and like the angels. Imagine for a moment the difference in energy between what you are now and what, for example, early man, the cave man was. We do not exaggerate when we tell you that it is an even greater step you are now coming to. This will open out for you a totally new perception of life, the meaning of life, the growth of life and the ability to soar to greater heights on all levels of existence.

We do not exaggerate, dear children. That is what is happening. There is no purpose in it as you understand purpose. It is to a large extent because of a natural progression, a natural development, and it is also because of the winds blowing. You will see for yourselves this new reality, a new perception that will be dazzling to you. You are nearly there. We have already explained why we cannot speak of exact dates and figures, but we can say that within the next few years you will be left in no doubt.

Shine forth, dear angels of Light. The experience you are walking towards is beyond your present comprehension. It is an opening of the mind that you cannot achieve with any drug or any physical stimulation. It is an opening of the mind, not just of intelligence, but of surreal perception

VIII. COMPREHENSION

We wish to talk about the energy you are in touch with in ourselves. Earlier we described it to you as "Original Thought". You find it almost impossible to understand anything that has no beginning or end, and because of your perceptions of birth and death, it is very difficult for us to describe the Energy. We ourselves are pure energy, energy that has always been in existence, but have evolved since part of our energy was set free. We have spoken to some extent of what happened to the energy set free, but we have not spoken of what happened to us.

At the time when part of the energy was set free it was pure energy. We cannot describe it as consciousness as such: it was a simple beingness. Through the soul-energies' repeated evolution by incarnation and subsequent return to the Source, the Original Thought has changed and this has grown consciousness within us. We use the terms 'us' and 'we' because there is not just one mass on our level. It is one, but it is made up of many parts. We could say it is like our ocean being made up of many drops of water.

So the Original Thought has progressed; we cannot say it is strengthened or more powerful - but there has been a stimulating process with each new intake of a drop returning the energy that you call the soul. When these drops of energy come back, they bring with them their experience of the Earth or wherever else they came from.

Before some of the original energy was set free there was a unity of energy, a fluidity of energy, but it was not a consciousness. We find this very difficult to put in your terms; perhaps it is easier to say we were pure Light, pure thought. We still are pure Light, pure thought, but enriched by the consciousness and the experiences that these many 'drops' of the soul have brought back to us.

You may wonder why there was this original separation and freeing. It may sound strange to you to talk of it as an 'automatic' process, but that is the best way to describe it. It was not a decision with a plan or a purpose. It was more an automatic or inevitable evolution of the Original Thought.

The vastness of energy to which you are linked is still beyond your comprehension. You wonder where it is and how it exists. If we were to tell you that it is all around you, that it exists everywhere, you would perhaps find this even harder. You have heard people talk of heaven but heaven, dear children, is all around you. We are all around you, we are everywhere. We are not just in the sky, we are not many Light years away. We are here and we are many Light years away.

At this time we are very close. We are closer perhaps than we have ever been. This, as we have tried to describe to you, is partly to do with the magnetism of the heightening energies within your globe, and it is in part to do with this pushing, blowing wind. You have your heaven upon Earth: it is the constant breathing in and breathing out of energies, attractions and magnetism.

You now understand the concept of higher energies returning in due course to what you call the God-Source. What has not perhaps occurred to you, dear children, is that it is through this line of attraction that we have come closer to you. We are not nebulous, not are we distant: we are here. We have always been here. We cannot say why - we just are, in purity and Light. But, dear children, you have enriched us, you have helped our own evolution, our growth of consciousness. There are things on your globe which you do not see, hear or taste, but they are there. We are here.

Every living thing emanated from the Original Thought. If you take one drop from your ocean many, many miles away, you would still say that that drop was part of that ocean - and so it is with you and the Thought.

Exciting things are occurring for you now. Watch, listen and be aware of them. There is almost a tingling of energies around you and if you had the eyes to see, around your channeller there is a vibratory energy of Light with sound imperceptible to you - a lightness, a tinkling sound. If we were in any way to force our energy through her, or any of you, there would be death. So our attraction to you at this time is like a gentle prodding, a stimulus. It is happening to everyone to a degree appropriate to the individual's own energy. It is an 'electrifying' time.

We have already spoken to you of the various implications of the energy within the individual. We do want to enlarge on that. It is all to do with attraction of energies - magnetism between the energy of the individual and ourselves. There have been short periods in your time when we were drawn towards one particular group or culture on the Earth, but we have never been so close to the whole globe. However, within a few years there will be a natural withdrawal of our stimulus from you as your own energy becomes such that it supports itself. We will break off the link and retreat from you. Yet in another sense we will always be around you as you evolve and travel on.

You have wanted to paint pictures to identify and clarify our relationship. You have wanted to analyse it into neat little sections and place them in separate boxes. Most of all you have wanted to name it. Now you must look instead at the greater force, the greater energy without those limitations. There is a stirring towards this in your mind; the molecules, the cells are being stimulated.

The most difficult task for you now is to leave your emotions, even if that sounds rather frightening. You have spoken much about love: "dying for love, killing for love". Love in its real sense is pure energy, and in the truest sense we ourselves ARE love - but we do not have emotions. Remember, dear children, you can and will be like us and you can be strong. You are getting stronger by the minute.

There will come about for you a new knowingness and a kind of perception in everybody which at present you call 'psychic'. Through it you will know each other directly - each other's needs, each other's strength - and when the transition is over, you will understand each other in a way you have never done before. There will be no need to desire to help, or feel you must help; you will know when and how to help. That is the age of knowingness.

We have already talked of greater perception of the senses. There will also be greater perception in understanding. Some of you will be highly telepathic. This will work by energies from within the thinking mind of another as a kind of code, entering your brain as Light, as thought, and being decoded there. So you will think each other's thoughts. This will mean that gradually you will have less need to talk, and eventually there will come a time when you will talk no more. When there is no further use for an instrument, it disintegrates.

Some of you already experience this advanced kind of telepathy, although you do not see it as such. You just feel the energy within your brain being 'churned up'. You have not quite reached the point where your brain will decode these messages and so they are rather jumbled. Some of you have been experiencing some quite strong head pains and this is the main cause of them. It is not just the pull of the magnetism between yourselves and the greater energy; it is also to do with the exchange of messages one to another. You can think of your mind energies as transporters of a kind, and your brains as stations where other thoughts coming to you arrive. When you begin to 'hear' in your mind this type of thought from others, it will be only that of a higher level of energy.

There is always an interaction between you, dear children. There always has been. It is the interaction between one level of energy and another. Some of you have already understood the interaction of the lower level of energy, of sympathy. Now we are talking to you of a higher interaction - the interaction of the mind. But as with anything new, you have to get used to it. Do not try to restrict that process. If you try to condense it, you will give yourself unnecessary pain. Instead, adjust your attitude to one of willingness, totally lacking fear, so that you open to the new energy readily - and then you will have opened the right frequency channel.

There have always been many ideals in your world, and many heroic actions and words spoken in the name of those ideals and in the name of love. Now you have the means, dear children, to make these ideals come true, although you will not achieve them out of desire but from strength and from the new 'instrument of the mind'.

You may ask why all this is proving such a rapid, almost harsh experience. Each different stage of evolution has been just as harsh in its own way and time for the individual to live through. Think of the change from lower, primitive man to compassionate man. You would surely say that that was a great leap, and so is the one that is occurring now, perhaps even greater.

You see, once you have uncovered your soul from its heavy cloak of fear, negative thought, hatred and wrong desire, it will expand at a rapid pace so that it can take this giant leap which is as much to do with the mind as anything else. Imagine for a moment, dear children, how much your negativity closed your minds. Imagine how as the 'curtain' of negativity is now pulled aside what a difference the Light makes pouring in, and how through that the soul can truly now join with the greater energy, with Original Thought.

We have referred to ourselves as part of Original Thought because we have always existed and because we are an energy that you can comprehend as thought, but we could just as easily and correctly call it Original Light or Original Love.

The number of changes which will occur because of the opening of the mind-energies is really beyond your belief. Part of the reason why so great an event is able to occur at this time is because your physical bodies are so strong. Over many generations you have built up immunities and strengths out of illness and disease, and you have great knowledge of what keeps your body strong. Such an occurrence as the present one happening to early man would undoubtedly have destroyed him. But of course it was not appropriate then because his physical energies were relatively low.

We have spoken before of the uniqueness of the human being, and we emphasize again, dear children, what a wonderful experience life is for you. We know this because throughout evolution, when a soul comes back and joins us in the ocean of the Source, it brings us understanding of the experience of the body. There is a change now of the cells in the body and there is a strengthening of the energy that encloses the body which will strengthen the bones and the muscles. There are some whose cell structure will 'blow out', and for them there will be some illness of the bones.

You may wonder what happens to those who cannot raise themselves up in order to open to the greater energy. Because this energy is now all around you it will affect even those of lower energy, but if their fear is so great that it causes bodily disturbances, then they will become ill and may even die. This is not a retribution, but it is a sadness. We speak of sadness not as emotion, but rather as a disappointment. Even so, there is nothing that can be done.

However, once again all of you have a very real opportunity to allow this great metamorphosis to come about and that is why we have spoken so much to you of fear and negative energy. Only when they have departed can the metamorphosis occur.

With some people of lower energy there is nothing that can be said which will make them let go of their cloak of fear. We cannot tell how many because, as we say, everyone has the opportunity. However, dear children, there will come a time when their opportunity is lost and they will have to depart from your world, because the new generation will all have a higher energy of soul. In that way there will be a clearing away once more of the old to bring in the new.

We speak of ourselves as being without emotion, but we do enjoy you. We love your happiness, your courage, your strength of spirit. We love your music, your creativeness. We have a kind of feeling towards you - it is hard for us to describe - a feeling without emotion. Perhaps it is best to call it perception.

We know that what we have just said touches a deep, clear note in your being. Yes, dear children, there is a purity of Light there. We could almost say we envy you its feeling of release, and of course it is not envy, but we do understand. If you feel it is what you have known deep down all your life, it is because that is true - for you and others like you. That is why we use the word 'awakening' - to what you knew at your origin. It is like coming from a heavy sleep, arising up into the Light and seeing the sun on a bright day.

We can comfort you, we can put our arms around you - the arms of understanding and the arms of truth. And we will say to you once more: you are free. You are Light. You are love.

IX. REALIZATION

Some of you are now in touch with the information we have given you and feel it to be true. If so, you have real understanding of what is happening. And some of you have come to a point of no return. The energies of the transition have been active over a long period of your time, but just as the over-fertile soil still needs the seed planted, water sprinkled on it to cause germination, and the sun to shine on it for growth, in themselves these words can do nothing. It is a whole experience of changed energies at this time that will give you the progress inherent in the transition. But our words can help you recognize circumstances.

After the period when the individual has awakened and blossomed like a flower, the predominating power and energy will be very different from before. The body will need time to get used to it and will very likely be the last thing to adjust, but once there is a synchronizing of the energies of mind, body and spirit, you will have strength and power probably beyond your wildest dreams.

Some of you are already aware that that means responsibility. Responsibility first and foremost to yourself; that must be your first consideration always. You must never take responsibility for another before yourself, and that includes even those who are weaker than you, those who are tiny or frail. Some of you will find this difficult to accept, but you cannot do it any more. If you do accept this and carry it out, then your vibrations will be so different that you will attract to you only those whom you *can* gently prod, advise and show the way forward.

You have been wondering whether you should try to teach people what you can understand. We can tell you that you cannot teach, you can only be there to advise gently and urge a little, but not push. In this way people who are drawn to you will know intuitively that you are the ones who understand, and contact you, sometimes in the most extraordinary way, even across whole continents or the globe. Very often those in need will be drawn to someone like you who is nearest in their vicinity, but sometimes the energy will attract across great distances, and you will hear people say, "I had to come more than 1,000 miles to find you.".

The whole structure of your being will be different, and with some of you it is already. So much - your taste, what you want, what you need, even what you feel - is different. There has been confusion with some people thinking that their very souls have been exchanged with another, but you are not really different people. It is just that as your energy is different, your very vibration is therefore very different and you feel it. Some of you will find that you do unusual things. You may want to go out walking in the middle of the night; you may find you wake up and crave a particular kind of food; you may find a need to wear a particular colour that you never wear. Go along with all these things, dear children. Do not resist, because none of your needs or wants will be wrong for you now. They cannot be wrong, because there is no such thing when the individual goes through the transition.

The only difficulty, dear children, is with those of lower energy, complacently going about their usual day-to-day life. You will find that they withdraw from you; not because they suddenly dislike you or feel uncomfortable with you (although some of them may), but they will withdraw without knowing why. They simply have the impulse running through them. Only those who have developed beyond that point will understand it.

We tell you these things now for comfort, in realization of truth. It is not just for those beginning their transition time, but also for those well on their way through it. It is not something that is easily imagined, and again only those who have experienced it can know that. Many of you can and do. We wish it could be all, but in reality we know that cannot be.

We paint you a picture of a Light cloud, so Light that it floats above the atmosphere. You, dear children, those passing through this experience, are like the Light cloud and those with lower energy are a dark cloud, dense and heavy. This does not represent good and evil, dear children - we emphasize that again. Some of you who succeed in this very important stage will have done some very negative things in the past; even what you may call evil things. That is not important here. A large proportion of you will have gone through or even perpetrated heavy experiences in their previous day-to-day life - tragedies, distress, terrors. Every experience is an opportunity to shake off fear and negativity, and that is why a large majority have had that kind of experience in your lives.

So there will be some who merit, "Well, they did some evil in the past, but they have now abandoned it." Judge not, dear children. This transition is nothing to do with good and evil, only to the extent that all negativities must be left behind.

We have told you before, and no doubt it still seems strange to you, that there will be a time when positive and negative will be no more, in fact all will be positive. There will be only Light. There is a time to maintain a balance, and then comes a time to move forward. You are passing not out of reality, but into reality, and although we will speak of a different reality, this does not mean that it is false or an illusion. Your reality on Earth, of the balance of day and night, Light and darkness, will go, because out of the transition those differences will be removed.

Again we speak of responsibility; the cloak of responsibility that is very definitely on the shoulders of those who pass through. We have been very careful not to give you names of people and not to talk too much of levels or gods, because these things would become restrictions for you. What we will say, dear children, is that after this time you will most certainly be as gods yourselves and that you will realize it.

Perhaps some of you can now begin to see why there need not be a hierarchy, why although there will still be leaders of a kind for practical reasons, you will all join together in a direct inner knowing of what must be done, and this will apply throughout your globe. There will be a global 'knowingness'. Now perhaps you can understand why there will be no wars. There will be no need for them. We have already tried to impart to you the sense you will have of the knowingness - the realization of each other's true needs which will be the norm. Perhaps these words will be like rain sprinkling on to the plants to help them grow.

You must, dear children, look now - look and see and realize if you can what is all around you. Perhaps the best way to understand the great change is to look at your children. They are growing in different soil; this has been noticed by many. There is a different type of child being born, and there are and will be more than the usual number of child deaths, perhaps at birth or a few months after while they are adjusting; some will fail then and will 'drop out'.

These words will not touch those of low energy. They will not reach them, so the information has been given largely to those with at least some understanding. We cannot teach you. We cannot write on a blackboard an alphabet of truth. That is only within you. Remember, all knowledge is within you.

The soul's journey has been a long one. There has been so much suffering, tragedy, disillusion. At last your souls are emerging out of darkness and into Light. There is no turning back. None of you need fear that you might turn the clock back again. Too much transformation of energy has already occurred. It can only go on expanding and changing into Light.

We use and have always used to you words that you can understand. Some they have been over-simplifications; sometimes they have been analogies. But they are all we can do (and we have done all we can) to bring through the truth for which you long.

We must talk now of the emotional aspect of this change. For those who take in the new energy like a sudden flash of Light, it will be extremely confusing. To some extent the emotions will be heightened at first, but the energy that is approaching cannot work with the emotions. We do not ask you to excise them, but to look in particular at negativity and fear. We are trying to say this gently, but what you need to understand is that most of your emotion is not sympathetic, or what you would call loving, but purely fear or negativity. Emotion is a kind of negativity.

However, it is also a two-sided coin, for some of you can raise yourselves up to a certain degree by heightening your emotion. If used sensibly the emotions can be a springboard for you. They cannot take you all the way; and there will be a point where you will have to leave them behind like a vehicle that no longer works. We do not demand any of this from you, not do we plead for it. We only speak in truth and for illumination, and every soul, every individual is free to take the opportunity - or to walk away. There will be no retribution or judgement for those who do not go forward. If we could describe ourselves as an emotion we could only say that we are love, and that we always love - all of you.

Some of you will be beginning now to understand this love without emotion, but for those of you who have not reached this point yet, we ask you to examine your emotions and discover what they really are, and, dear children, be honest with yourselves. Don't hide within the negativity of desire or fear. Look! Some of the emotions are bred into you almost genetically. We speak of those emotions you would call instinct: the usual instant love between mother and child, for instance. That will not die. Do not fear that you will somehow cut yourself off from love.

We want to break down all the defences, barriers and the structures you have built up, not for destruction's sake but because on breaking down those barriers you will be able to see further, you will be able to see everywhere. But what we know is right is of no consequence in itself because the general energy current is escalating in any case, even now, and accelerating of its own volition.

Some of you feel that you should try to heal the world. Dear children, the world is not yours to heal. But of course you can by your own beacons of Light be golden rays in the world. This does not require you to think, or sit in long meditations to project this Light, although you can do this if you want to and it will not be wasted. Again we tell you that there is no responsibility to anyone more important than your own responsibility to yourself. You can do every bit as much by just being. Be, dear children, *be!* We see you at this moment as beacons of Light, golden Light shining brightly all around you. Know that that is what you are and you will be healers of the world.

Some of you have been most concerned about the planet, the Earth and the trees and creatures that live on it. Things are changing rapidly. It is sometimes only by destruction that the futility and the pointlessness of it is learned. By all means pray, dear children, for your globe, but what is happening is happening rightly, even the destruction.

Over the last hundred years on your globe you have had enormous upheavals, tremendous destruction, famines and wars on a scale that has never occurred before. All these things were a break-up of the old for the new to enter, and all have been opportunities for the Light in man to transcend the darkness. It is the Light in you that makes you healers - the golden Light which emanates from you because of your inner truth.

X. ARRIVAL

We come to you with joy and with love. We have endeavoured to impart information to you to lay a strong foundation for the growth of the individual, which is the key factor in this important transition time.

By now many of you will be going through or have gone through your own changes, and will really be able to relate to what we say. The whole subject, beingness itself, is so very vast, dear children, and yet we tell you truly, it is so very simple.

We have tried to put this information clearly and succinctly. We understand that each different channeller, each different individual must bring a quality of their own into the words because, as we have described before, channelling is a synthesis and each truth given will have the imprint of the individual on it. There is a vast number of people at this time who can relate to higher truth through channelling, not to be teachers of the world, but primarily to be teachers of themselves.

We wish to speak a little about the male and female principles. Most of you readily understand that within an individual there is not just male or female - there are both, genetically and physically. When the soul has been uncovered from the cloak of negativity and the spirit-energy rises within the individual, he becomes aware of many learning processes. Sometimes he is suddenly bombarded by a lightning flash of truth; at others it is more gentle. It depends on the individual. There comes a certain point when the energy of the individual's gender has to be looked at. If it is a man, he has to look at his masculine principles: his aggression, for instance, his dominance, his power. If it is a female, she has to look at the principles of femininity: submission, inspiration and compassion. Then, dear children, as in all things they need to take up the opposite of that innate gender and there will be a blending within each of the two forces, male and female, positive and negative. When that transformation happens that individual is then above the physical principle of sexuality and has come to a balance and a completeness within him or herself.

This blending of principles, male and female, positive and negative, has already begun. When the individuals have risen above it they really are able to link with their god within and the god without. Such blending is even going on in a physical sense at this time. Most of you understand that the world functions on the interaction of the positive and negative principles. Now, put simply, there is a powerful realization of them which will result in many of you rising beyond it.

Some of you have felt as though you are riding uphill on a difficult bicycle. The peak of the transition is like the top of the hill. We cannot say that having reached it the individual will then feel totally free of all earthly feeling; but there will indeed be a release and liberation. Dear children, this is a tremendous time for you because in the past year only a few people have accomplished the transition. Now, dear children, there will be many, many souls dropping away the dark curtain of their fears and doubts, allowing the purity of their inner Light to soar and join with the God-Source and Truth.

Do not concern yourselves over those who cannot see all this. We said previously that there will be a marked difference between those of you who undertake the transition and those who have no inclination for it. Remember that evolution is a never-ending process for all. We hope now that you see and understand.

We have not spoken to you of specific disasters and physical destruction. You first approached us wanting to know of these things and although, in truth, dear children, there will be as we have said a breaking down, a collapse of regimes and physical disintegration around your globe, you must remember that no energy from any soul is ever wasted. Our words are not of destruction, but of hope and of joy.

We would like to paint you a picture. Imagine an ordinary Light in an ordinary room. Over the Light is a dark, dark cloak. Individuals have had to grope and feel their way around the dark room, stumbling without Light to guide them as they searched for the way out and failed to find it. They have looked everywhere but to themselves. They have stumbled, strutted and groped around. They have collapsed in a heap, despondent and despairing. But finally, through acceptance of themselves, through inner realization dawning as they sat there in the dark room, they have discovered how simple the answer is: they have merely to reach out, lift the edge of the cloak (which is your own darkness) and immediately the Light is there. Dear children, the Light has always been there for you, but you have not seen it.

This transition period on your globe is not, as we have said, something completely new, but the scale of it is, and that is truly wonderful. It is not just about the individual's growth: there is also the cosmic wind blowing. But you do not need to concern yourself with the cosmic wind. Concern yourself with and look only to yourselves, because that is where your truth lies and always has. If you do you will see many light bulbs appear around your globe and you will begin to look through new eyes in perfect Light. Imagine that, dear children, and see and know now that this change, this transition time is truly one of illumination.

Think of silk worms weaving their silk, their cocoons. Then think of the chrysalis inside, dark but growing. And then think of the cocoon being broken out of and the ensuing flight that takes place. You can understand this analogy.

There are no particular exercises for you to carry out, although we have imparted one or two ideas to you. There is no one thing to do. There is no one Messiah to follow. There is only you and your Light. We hope you have understood our words.

Our connection to you is not over now. There has been on your part both a desire to know truth and a desire to join your truth to the highest truth, and although our dialogues together are coming to an end now, know that this link between us is always there and will emerge whenever you send us your thoughts, because your Light and our Light can be and are joined. Do not be concerned that you may not 'get it right'. We cannot say to you that everything you do will be perfect. But as long as you open to the truth, the truth is there for you.

And we say this to all. Know that you are bodies of Light. Know your strengths, because your weaknesses will disappear. Trust your Light and be guided by it; accept your responsibility for yourself. You are alone, but you are one with God. And most of all, dear children, accept...   *Accept your destiny.*